Hide and Seek
Jazzy's Alphabet Adventure

by
Sonja McGiboney

Copyright January, 2022

Jazzy closed her eyes,
And promised not to peek
While the letters ran away
For their game of hide-and-seek!

A hid with the apples,

B stayed by the ball;
Bo

C rested with the cat,

And D hid with a doll.

E stood by the eggs,

F behind a feather;

G ran in the garden,

And H jumped in the heather.

I hid near the ice cream,

J enjoyed the jam;

K floated on a kite,

And L sat with a lamb.

15

M hid near a mailbox,

N read all the news;

O stood near the oranges,

And Phid in the pews.

Q hid on the quarter,

R went on the road;

S sat on the stairs with stars

And T stood by a toad.

U hid under the umbrella,

V v on the vibraphone;

W stood on the window sill,

and X on the xylophone.

Y hid with a ball of yarn,

And **Z** in the Zebra's pen;

And when the game was over,
They napped in Jazzy's den!

Sonja McGiboney grew up in Stowe, Pennsylvania. After obtaining her undergraduate degree in music from West Virginia University, she married Dale and accompanied him on his 25-year military career. She has two wonderful children, Rachel and Ryan, and now lives with Dale and Jazzy in Smithfield, Virginia. She loves taking photos and writing Jazzy's Books.

Check out all Jazzy's books!

1. ABC Jazzy
2. Counting Down Jazzy
3. Growing Up Jazzy
4. Hide and Seek - Jazzy's Alphabet Adventure
5. Jazzy and Friends
6. Jazzy Colors
7. Jazzy Time
8. Jazzy Shapes
9. Jazzy Explores the Library
10. Jazzy Explores Smithfield, VA
11. Jazzy Explores Murfreesboro, NC
12. Jazzy's Halloween - A Night in Ghouling Brook
13. Jazzy's Twelve Days of Christmas
14. Little Red Jazzyhood
15. Princess Jazzy - How to Prove You're a Princess

Printed in the USA
CPSIA information can be obtained
at www.ICGtesting.com
LVHW062103031123
762998LV00021B/979